Looking at IRAN

Shopping in the bazaar

سالن آرایش و زیبایی
باغچه بان
آرایشگاه باغچه بان
ویژه بانوان

Looking at
IRAN

Written and Photographed by
JANINE WIEDEL

Adam and Charles Black   London

J. B. Lippincott Company   Philadelphia and New York

Many Iranian women wear a veil called
the *chador* when they appear in public

Looking at Other Countries

Looking at HOLLAND	**Looking at SWEDEN**
Looking at ITALY	**Looking at GERMANY**
Looking at GREECE	**Looking at GREAT BRITAIN**
Looking at NORWAY	**Looking at BRAZIL**
Looking at DENMARK	**Looking at CHINA**
Looking at JAPAN	**Looking at NIGERIA**
Looking at SPAIN	**Looking at CANADA**
Looking at FRANCE	**Looking at AUSTRALIA**
Looking at ISRAEL	**Looking at RUSSIA**

Further titles in preparation

The photographs in this book were taken by the author, with
the following exceptions:

British Library 43b
J. Allan Cash Ltd 8b, 32a and c, 50a, 55, 57
Mary Evans Picture Library 16
John Free 7a
Robert Harding Associates 7b, 38a, 46, 50b (John G. Ross)
Alan Hutchison Library 31 (Sarah Errington), 38b, 47
Iranian Tourist and Information Centre 45b, 48b, 49a and b
Sotheby Parke Bernet Inc. 34a
Suzanne Wiedel-Pace **51**

The map on page 63 was prepared by Mark Foxall

The cover pictures show (a) a nomad mother and baby (b) wall
decoration in an Isfahan mosque

US Library of Congress Cataloging in Publication Data

Wiedel, Janine.
    Looking at Iran.

    (Looking at other countries)
    Includes index
    SUMMARY: An introduction to the history, geography, economy, culture, and
people of the land that used to be known as Persia.
    1. Iran—Juvenile literature. [1. Iran] I. Title.
DS254.4.W48   1978   955'05   78-6038
ISBN-0-397-31797-2

ISBN 0 7136 1806 X

© 1978 A & C BLACK (PUBLISHERS) LIMITED, 35 BEDFORD ROW,
LONDON WC1R 4JH

FIRST PUBLISHED 1978

PRINTED IN GREAT BRITAIN BY MORRISON & GIBB LTD, EDINBURGH

CONTENTS

An Iranian family

The Land

Iran is a Middle Eastern country. Throughout its history Iran, or Persia as it used to be called, has been a land bridge between west and east. It has the Arab world, Turkey and Europe to the west and Central Asia and India to the east. To the north is the Caspian Sea, the largest inland lake in the world. Most of the Caspian Sea lies inside the Soviet Union. To the south of Iran is the Persian Gulf, a shallow landlocked stretch of sea separating Iran from the Arabian peninsula.

Iran's geographical position has meant that throughout history people going by land from Europe to Asia have had to cross Iran. Traders followed the three main routes of the Ancient World which passed through it, carrying merchandise such as silk from China to the Near East and Europe. This constant flow of different peoples, some just passing through and others coming to settle in the country, helped Persian civilization and culture to develop. But invading armies also followed the trade routes and so the country was vulnerable to attack and conquest by other nations.

The shade is a welcome relief from the scorching heat of the sun

A grove of date palms
near Shiraz

Weeding the crops in one of the
many newly irrigated areas

Iran is about the same size as France, Great Britain, Spain, Italy and Switzerland combined, or more than twice the size of Texas.

It is one of the highest countries in the world. Most of the land, except for narrow strips along the coast, lies on a high plateau with an average height of four to five thousand feet (1200 to 1500 m) above sea level. Three main mountain ranges —the Zagros to the west, the Makran to the south and the Elburz to the north—cut across the plateau.

Between April and November the sun beats down relentlessly. Summer then changes rapidly into winter and the bitter cold arrives. The total rainfall throughout the year on the plateau is only two to ten inches (50 to 250 mm). There is plenty of rain along the Caspian coast where wheat, barley, sugar cane and tea are grown, but the rest of Iran is mostly arid.

Throughout history Iran has supplied water to its dry regions by complicated systems of dams, canals and *qanats*. A

This vast plateau is the typical landscape of much of Iran

qanat is an underground tunnel, sometimes as much as sixty miles (100 km) long, which carries water from a natural reservoir in water-bearing rock, deep underground in the mountains, to a town or village in a dry area. The water flows from the reservoir along the qanat and comes to the surface just above the village. The water obtained in this way is used for drinking and for irrigating fields, gardens and orchards which make a vivid patch of green in the brown of the surrounding countryside. When a new qanat is being constructed, the builders dig shafts along the chosen route and then tunnel from shaft to shaft. The dirt from the tunnel is hauled up the shafts in baskets and dumped around the heads of the shafts.

Iranian skill in making the best use of a limited water supply made it possible in the past for the country to support a great civilization. Today modern technology is bringing water to an even wider area, but water is still a very precious commodity that has to be paid for.

A *qanat* can be traced on the surface by the mounds of earth left by the builders

Life in the City

An Iranian city wakes up at five o'clock in the morning, the streets echoing with a wide variety of songlike shouts. Men in baggy trousers with lengths of cloth over their shoulders, or boxes of all shapes and sizes piled on their heads, wake the sleeping people to sell them their wares. Some offer bread or fruit, others newspapers. Figures begin to appear from the houses, in doorways or leaning from their windows, trying to catch the passing trader who can sell them bread, still hot from the oven, and tea, not in packets but weighed out on the spot, for the morning meal. Even a new suit of clothes can be bought for the new day.

Government offices and banks open between seven and seven-thirty in the morning. By eight o'clock schools have already begun the day's lessons and shopkeepers are rolling up their heavy wooden or metal shutters. They water down the cobbled pavements in front of their shops, to wash away the previous day's dirt.

Many of the shops are very small and the goods are displayed neatly on the ground in front of the shop. Some have mountains of green melons or yellow bananas, others have rows of knives and forks spread out on patterned cloths or Persian carpets. Shopkeepers who sell fabrics and carpets pile them roll upon roll, hang them from the rafters, spread them before you, twisting them backwards and forwards in the

Nearly everything can be bought from a passing seller

A mobile hardware shop

9

Most shops have open fronts and display their wares to the passers-by

sun. In the deep shadows of the shop they show you the richness of the intricate designs, bedazzle you with the variety and bargain over the price.

In the streets there are not only men in business suits and women in skirts and dresses but also dark figures in long, flowing, all-enveloping veils. These are women who follow the ancient Islamic belief that the female figure should not be seen in public. They wear a special veil, the *chador*. This is a sheet of cotton material, usually black, plain or patterned, which is draped over the head and hangs shapelessly down to the feet, sometimes leaving only the eyes visible.

It is not unusual to see two women walking together, one dressed in modern fashion, the other in a chador. But, if the chador is blown back, it can be seen that beneath it the veiled lady's dress is just as fashionable as her friend's.

This is one example of something very common in Iran. Some people live, dress and work in much the same way as their counterparts in Europe and America, but others choose a more traditionally Iranian way of life. They accept some of the ideas and influences that come from abroad but reject others.

In Tehran, the capital city of Iran, the streets and pavements are some of the busiest of any city. The roads are filled with vehicles of every size and shape; alongside modern trucks and cars, mostly imported from Europe or America, are

A modern shopping complex

Pedestrians take their lives in their hands when crossing through Iranian traffic

Sheep and traffic mingle on city streets

dilapidated bicycles, some carrying two or three people at once, and horse-drawn carts loaded to overflowing.

In Tehran there are wide eight-lane boulevards, carefully timed traffic lights, complicated intersections and one-way systems to keep the traffic moving smoothly. But many drivers ignore the rules and go the wrong way up a street or slam on their brakes without warning.

Pedestrians face another hazard: the wide ditch or *djub* which runs along the street. In the past this ditch provided the only water supply for the houses, apart from drinking water which was distributed on handcarts. The water was released into the djubs only on certain days, and, as soon as it was running clear, householders would use it to fill up the storage tanks in their houses. Today the djubs are used mainly for removing refuse and for

LEFT The water channel which runs along most streets in Iranian cities. RIGHT The water is used for a variety of purposes

keeping alive the trees that shade the streets. However, it is not uncommon to see poorer women, who do not have running water in their homes, washing dishes or clothes in these ditches.

Most shops and offices are closed between twelve and four in the afternoon when the heat is fiercest. Some people go home, others stay in their offices or go to restaurants, while others use the pavements or sidewalks for resting and eating. The street traders of the early morning are once again active, but this time they are surrounded by a hungry crowd. The foods sold in the streets vary from season to season. Summer brings delicacies such as hot boiled beetroots covered with a delicious sweet syrup. In winter there is corn on the cob, cooked while you wait. At all times of the year there are thick soups cooked on the spot and ladled into small tin bowls.

Boiled beetroots are a popular snack

Tea and tobacco at midday

Asleep in the shade

After their meal men can be seen in most streets, stretched out on the ground sound asleep on neatly spread newspapers, often with other newspapers over their faces to keep out the roasting heat of the summer sun. Inside a closed shop you might see the outline of the shopkeeper, lying restfully on top of the counter. Iranians seem to have the ability to fall asleep anywhere, once the midday heat arrives.

At four o'clock the city wakes up for the second time. Shop fronts reopen and the business of buying and selling begins again. Most shops shut by seven or eight in the evening, but food shops remain open much later.

Traditionally the evening meal is a family gathering and a time for discussing the events of the day. The art of conversation is important to Iranians. In the past men used to meet regularly

Women meet their friends in the courtyard of a mosque, the Muslim place of worship

Smoking a hubble-bubble

at one another's houses for conversation. This tradition is still kept up by many today.

The main places for people to meet their friends outside the home are in the courtyards of mosques during the times of prayer and in the streets and teahouses. Another popular meeting place is the *hammam* or baths where clients undergo a rigorous steaming, showering, massage and scraping as well as a good soaping. Women have their own section of the baths, shut off from that of the men. For both men and women a visit to the baths is an outing during which they can meet their friends and relax with tea and conversation.

Along with tea and companionship goes the famous hubble-bubble pipe. It is so designed that the smoke from the burning tobacco in the bowl of the pipe passes through water. In this way the smoke is cooled before it reaches the mouth. When smoking a hubble-bubble, one is supposed to forget all the worries of life.

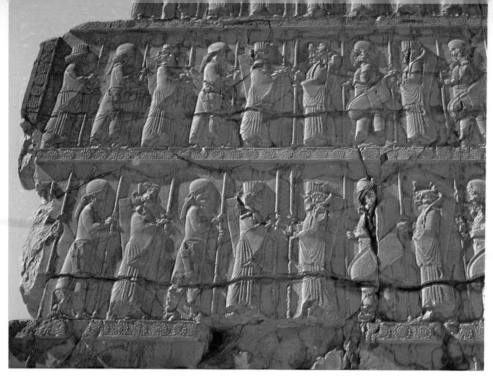

A Now Ruz or New Year procession of 2500 years ago, carved on
a staircase at Persepolis

Religion

Throughout the ages religion has pervaded nearly every aspect
of Persian life. The first national religion of Persia was Zoroastrianism. Its prophet, Zoroaster, lived some time between
1000 and 800 BC. He taught that the world was a battleground
between the forces of good and evil. After death the soul's
fate was decided by the precise balance between the good and
bad deeds performed during life. Fire was considered the source
of life, and so fire worship was an important part of Zoroastrian
ritual. Fire temples were often built over seepages of natural gas.

The Iranian New Year festival, Now Ruz, dates from
Zoroastrian times. It begins on March 21—the spring equinox
when days and nights are the same length—and ends on April 2.
On New Year's Day the Shah, the ruler of Iran, holds an official
reception as his predecessors did in Zoroastrian times. Throughout Iran everyone who can wears new clothes and a special meal
is served made up of seven things beginning with the letter "s".

It is a time for visiting friends and picnicking in the spring sunshine.

Zoroastrianism still exists in Iran, as do other faiths, but the official religion today, and that of ninety-five per cent of Iranians, is Islam (the word means "submission to God"). It was founded by Muhammad in Arabia in the early part of the seventh century AD. Its followers are called Muslims. They believe that the angel Gabriel brought Muhammad a message from God. This was written down in a sacred book called the Koran which contains all the laws and regulations by which Muslims are to perfect their lives. The essential Muslim beliefs are that there is only one God and that Muhammad is his prophet and that it is a believer's duty to pray five times a day, to fast from dawn to dusk in the holy month of Ramadan, to help the poor with charity and, if possible, to make the pilgrimage to Mecca, the holy city of Islam.

The Persians were converted to Islam in the seventh century AD by invading Arab armies. Within a few years they showed their independence by forming a separate party within Islam called Shia. Unlike other Muslim denominations, the followers of Shia Islam venerate Muhammad's grandsons, two martyrs called Hassan and Hosein. They are remembered each year during Muharram, the month of mourning. There are services

The courtyard of a mosque, a place of prayer and repose for Muslims

and processions and, in some places, passion plays re-enacting the deaths of the martyrs.

As Hosein and his followers tried to fight off their enemies in the desert, they suffered terribly from thirst. In memory of that, religious Iranians give money to charitable societies which distribute free water to the needy. On many streets in Iran one sees *sakkahanehs* which are large tanks filled with water. Metal cups hang from them and passers-by may drink freely.

Shia Islam is brought to the people by *mullahs*, men trained in the study of the Koran. In the past they provided the only education available for children and young men. They administered the Koranic law and also had a strong voice in political events. In recent years much of their power has been taken away by the government because it was felt that their influence was preventing Iran from developing into a modern country.

A Muslim must pray five times a day, before sunrise, after midday, in the late afternoon, at sunset and when it is dark. On Friday, the Islamic holy day, men must say the midday prayers in a mosque. On other days they may say them anywhere, but many men choose to visit the mosque throughout the week.

LEFT A *sakkahaneh*. The metal hand commemorates a hero whose hands were cut off when he tried to obtain water for Hosein. RIGHT A mullah

Before and after praying there is time for meeting friends or even for falling asleep in the mosque courtyard

Praying in one of the niches reserved for prayer

Before praying a Muslim must purify himself by a symbolic wash, often using the water from the pools in the mosque courtyard. Then he removes his shoes and enters one of the open niches provided around the walls of the courtyard. When he prays he must face in the direction of Mecca. He marks out a small space at his feet. This isolates him from the outer world. Sometimes the space is defined by a small carpet which he thinks of as the extent of his world into which no one intrudes. A Muslim praying is totally involved in his communion with God.

A man begins to pray by standing with his arms outstretched in front and pronouncing the words "God is great". Then he lowers his arms and recites some prayers. Still standing, he bows deeply, his palms on his knees, straightens up and then, finally, lies full length, his nose to the ground.

Women usually pray at home. They recite the same prayers and perform the same actions as the men.

In the month of Ramadan Iranian Muslims, like those of other denominations, fast during the hours of daylight in memory of the giving of the Koran to Muhammad. When dusk comes, everyone rushes to find something to eat.

A fruit and vegetable market

Food

The staple diet of Iran is bread, rice, cheese and home-made yogurt. A wider variety is available to those who can afford it. The new supermarkets sell tinned and packaged food, but most people still prefer the traditional Persian dishes of meat cooked in a variety of ways and served with rice. The food is usually hot and spicy, so most main dishes are accompanied by a bowl of fresh yogurt to soothe the palate.

The national drink is tea, taken black without milk, and from a glass, not a cup. Drinks made from the fruits in season are sold both in the streets and in shops and restaurants. In hot weather a particularly popular one is made of water, vinegar, sugar and sliced cucumbers.

In bread shops one can see the bakers at work, kneading and shaping the dough and baking the bread in red-hot ovens where the loaves cook on top of hot pebbles. The new-baked bread, hot from the oven, is weighed before it is handed to the customer. The baker breaks off or adds a piece to obtain the exact weight the customer wants.

Each bread shop specializes in a particular type of loaf. Some kinds are flat and look like oversized pancakes. These are stacked as they come out of the oven and then are wrapped and put on the back of a bicycle, or on top of someone's head, to be sold from door to door. Another popular shape is long, flat and oval. These loaves are hung on pegs from the shop ceiling, awaiting sale.

Bread has to be weighed before it is sold

LEFT A round flat loaf before it is baked. MIDDLE A pile of flat loaves ready for delivery. RIGHT Long loaves hanging in the shop

Bread shops are cheerful places smelling deliciously of hot bread and are full of friendly chatter. Like most small shops, bread shops are generally family businesses, with the family living nearby and knowing most customers by name.

The main meats eaten are lamb and chicken. Sheep are herded daily through the streets and people can buy a live sheep and kill and butcher it themselves. It is not unusual, even in large cities, to see a whole sheep's carcass hanging from a tree outside a house, ready for cooking the same day.

Shish kebab is very popular and can be bought ready cooked. It is made by grilling pieces of lamb, green pepper and onion on skewers over hot coals. The meat is highly seasoned with spices. Kebab shops are open to the street and the customer can watch his meat being cooked.

Bread delivery

24

Grilling *shish kebab*

The melon seller

Fruit, one of Iran's exports, is an important part of the diet. Some fruits and nuts (the plum, almond and pistachio, for instance) are said to have originated in Persia.

A great range of fruit—apples, pears, peaches, apricots, grapes, cherries, quinces, dates—is grown in the irrigated parts of Iran, and oranges, lemons, melons and pomegranates are cultivated in the hot coastal areas of the Persian Gulf and Indian Ocean.

The melon and the pomegranate are very popular. It is said that, when the melon comes into season, an Iranian may eat ten to twelve pounds (about 5 kg) of melon a day for a fortnight. During the seventeenth century melons were taken

Fruit sellers

by men on foot all the way from Iran to the courts of India. The pomegranate is cherished because Muhammad, the founder of Islam, taught his followers that this fruit would purge them of all envy and hate.

Donkeys carrying great baskets of fruit can be seen on street corners or winding their way through the crowds. The fruit-seller weighs out some fruit and calls out a price, hoping to attract a customer. The donkey, the fruit seller and his scales are a miniature shop, always on the move.

Caviar, another major Iranian export to other countries, is too expensive for most Iranians. It is the oily roe of the sturgeon, a large fish caught in the Caspian Sea.

Bazaars

Bazaar is the Persian word for "market". But, unlike markets elsewhere, the Iranian bazaar is not just a place where goods are bought and sold. In the past the bazaar was the setting for important business meetings. Marriages were negotiated there, political moves planned, legal cases decided and international trade organized. The bazaar was a community with its own customs, laws and clan chieftains. At some periods its power was so strong that it could bring about the collapse of a government. Murmurings of discontent among the leaders of the bazaars usually foretold political crisis. Today the bazaars, though mainly used as shopping areas, still retain much of their past importance as places for meeting and discussing events.

Inside the bazaar

Mosques often open directly into the bazaar

Selling cooking oil by weight

Often the bazaar stands on the main square next to a mosque. Sometimes a mosque is found inside the bazaar, surrounded by goods for sale. This mingling of worship and business can be seen throughout Iran, for the Islamic religion does not separate the spiritual and material sides of life.

Entering a bazaar is like entering a vast honeycomb. Inside the gateway, in the darkness of the passageways, the dirt paths seem to lead on for ever beneath the high vaulted ceilings. Beautiful rays of light come streaming down through skylights pierced in the ceiling. Along both sides of the narrow path are booths, open-fronted shops and small cubbyholes barely more than niches scooped out of the wall. Each of these is filled with wares of some sort.

Coming into the darkness of the bazaar

A nomad family rests in the bazaar

Everywhere there are things for sale, from locally grown rice and spices to plastic dolls made in America.

At first the bazaar may seem to be laid out at random, but there is an overall plan. One lane resounds with the clanging noise of coppersmiths at work, another smells of rich spices. Round a corner a nomad tribesman is sitting on top of a large pile of brightly patterned rugs, waiting for customers.

Buying in a bazaar involves a form of game between buyer and seller. Nothing has a fixed price. The seller names a high price and the buyer replies by offering a very low one. After a long period of friendly argument, and perhaps a glass of tea, a price will be agreed upon, to the satisfaction of both buyer and seller.

A carpet seller. The brush will be used to show how fine the pile of the carpet is

Carrying loads. LEFT A nomad woman with her bundle. RIGHT A professional porter delivering a huge load

A craftsman decorating a copper dish

The bazaar is the place to find Iranian craftsmen at work. From very early times coppersmiths, weavers, goldsmiths and many other artisans have made and sold their wares in their workshops in the bazaar. Both the shops and the crafts have been handed down in the same families for generation after generation.

There is a continual flow of people along the dirt paths. One sees women with enormous bundles on their heads, men carrying heavy loads of every description, and donkeys piled high with goods. For those who buy more than they can possibly carry, there are professional porters for hire. No one appears to be wandering about aimlessly. Everyone seems to be moving to and fro with purpose.

Village Life

Although more and more people are moving into the cities, a large part of the Iranian population still lives in remote villages and settlements. These small communities exist wherever there is soil suitable for growing crops and water for drinking and irrigation. Most of the villages are totally self-supporting and many grow crops for export as well as for local use. Flocks of sheep and goats are part of the village scenery and provide wool and hair as well as meat and milk. Barley and wheat are the main cereal crops, though rice is also grown in the Caspian Sea provinces. Tobacco, tea and sugar beet are also cultivated in considerable quantities, and fruit trees are planted wherever the climate permits. Cotton fields provide the yarn for the lovely patterned Persian fabrics, and silkworm cocoons produce silk thread that is spun and woven on hand looms.

The farmers generally live in small, compact and often very crowded settlements or villages. A village is usually a network of narrow lanes bordered by high mud walls, with doorways leading to the courtyards of the houses. Most villages have one main street; along it runs the water channel which is the lifeline of the settlement.

Village houses are made of dried-mud bricks, except in the Caspian provinces where wood is more plentiful. The

Threshing grain in western Iran

A village in the desert regions of central Iran

Weaving a carpet. The pattern being followed is pinned to the loom

Wind towers trap the breeze and carry it down to the rooms inside the houses, to cool them during the summer months

interiors are very simple. The floors are generally of hard earth covered with rugs. At mealtimes the floor becomes the table as there are rarely any tables and chairs.

Work is clearly divided between men and women. The men till the fields, which are often a long way from the village, and the women look after the house, spin yarn and weave rugs. For relaxation after the day's work is over, the villagers drink tea, smoke and talk. It is during these evening hours that the ballads, folk tales and poetry for which Persians are traditionally famous are kept alive.

Villagers' contacts with the larger towns are generally limited to visits, with a heavily laden donkey, to sell basket-loads of straw, fuel, fruit or vegetables to the townsfolk. Occasionally the entire family may go into the nearest town for the day to shop in the bazaar. Some villages have shops but they sell only basic necessities such as tea, sugar, tobacco, rice and spices.

Artists and Craftsmen

Over a million people in Iran are engaged in handicrafts. Many work and sell in the bazaars, while others work at home or in small shops. They are still working very much in the traditions of the past. The modern patterns are somewhat less refined, but this is no doubt the effect of the tourist trade which now encourages craftsmen to turn out more work in less time. Throughout the ages Iranian artists have transformed everyday things such as beakers, bowls, lamps and rugs into works of art. Their art today, as in the past, is based on traditional patterns and designs which are very strongly linked with the Islamic religion.

Persian carpets have long been famous. In Iran, even the humblest home has one of these lovely rugs. The poor man eats his meals on it, sleeps on it and prays on it. The entire process of carpet making, beginning with the spinning of cotton and wool into yarn, is done by hand. The wool is steeped in vegetable dyes made from secret family recipes. The dyed skeins of wool are hung on racks to dry in the sunshine of a courtyard.

A coppersmith

A small boy learns his father's craft

Skeins of dyed wool
hanging out to dry

A fine silk carpet

For each rug a particular pattern is drawn up in advance
and followed carefully. The patterns come from everyday life.
Flowers, fruits, vegetables and animals are usually used,
alternating with arabesques (flowing lines of intertwined
branches, leaves and scrollwork).

Each region of Iran has its own particular range of dyes
and type and quality of rug. An expert can tell where a rug
comes from by examining the pattern, the dyes, and the type
and number of knots used. He can tell whether it has been made
in a nomad encampment, a village home or a city workshop or
factory.

Calligraphy, the art of handwriting, holds an important place in Persian life. The script, adopted from the Arabs, runs across the page from right to left, not from left to right as ours does. Consequently books have the spine on the right, and the pages are turned from left to right. It is fascinating to watch an Iranian write his beautiful flowing script—many marks, dots and dashes—moving his hand across the paper in what seems, to American and European eyes, to be the wrong direction. This script is worked into the pattern and design of most Persian art. Its importance lies both in the visual beauty of the written letter forms and in the meaning of the words, usually taken from the Koran.

Pages from an illustrated manuscript

Ever since the eleventh century Persians have been masters of miniature painting. These paintings are so tiny that often they are painted with a brush containing a single hair. They illustrate verses from the Koran, poetry or tales of kings and legendary heroes. The style and form have changed very little over the centuries. This is because young Iranians have always learned from older masters and, instead of trying to change the art, they have worked hard to follow and refine the old tradition.

35

Arabic script used as decoration

The mosque is perhaps the perfect example of the art of the past and of the merging of art and religion. Mosques are found in all countries where the Islamic faith spread, even as far west as Spain, but the Iranian mosque has its own individual style. The patterns which are used to decorate Iranian mosques are extremely intricate, and texts from the Koran are used freely to decorate the walls.

A mosque is a walled enclosure with an imposing gateway, usually flanked by two minarets or towers. One walks through the entrance and comes into an open courtyard, where there are pools of water, often surrounded by trees and flowers. On the side facing Mecca, the sacred city of the Islamic faith, an inner wall has an entrance leading into a sanctuary roofed by a dome. Arcades line the other walls of the courtyard. The entire mosque, inside and out, is covered with mosaics and brilliantly hued tiles.

The cupolas or domes of mosques are particularly magnificent in size and in richness of decoration. They appear on the skyline like huge turquoise bubbles. No two domes in the whole of Iran are exactly alike. They are all similar in style but their details differ. The decorations consist of geometric designs, floral motifs and Arabic script.

Tribal women LEFT and RIGHT Qashqai
MIDDLE Bakhtiari

Nomads

One sixth of the population of Iran is made up of nomads—
people who have no fixed settlements but who migrate every
year between their summer pastures in the mountains and their
winter pastures in the lowlands, in search of grass for their
flocks of sheep and goats. It is government policy to settle the
nomads permanently in villages but, until the vast areas of
arid land in Iran can be irrigated and developed to grow crops
all the year round, a nomadic way of life is the only means of
survival for this large section of the people.

Most nomads belong to tribes or groups such as the Kurds,
Lurs, Bakhtiari, Baluchi, Turkomans and Qashqai. Some tribes
are descended from very early inhabitants of the Iranian
plateau, others from Central Asian invaders; and some, like
the Qashqai, were brought in from outside Iran to serve as
a military force. With these varied origins it is not surprising
that the tribes speak a variety of languages and dialects which
cannot usually be understood by outsiders. Their portable
homes vary too. The Bakhtiari and Qashqai, for instance, have
tents made of black goat's hair, while the Turkomans make
theirs of felt.

37

The tribes played an important part in Persian history. They were independent of city-based government and their chieftains had considerable wealth. This came from settled villages which they owned, as well as from their huge flocks. Ambitious men, and even foreign governments, would try to win support for their political moves from an important tribe.

The men of the tribes are responsible for hunting and for tending the flocks, while the women do the cooking, sewing, spinning and weaving of fabric and rugs. The nomads are almost entirely self-sufficient. To obtain the few necessities that they cannot provide for themselves, they go into the towns to sell or barter sheep, milk, butter and rugs for town goods. The women's home-made dresses of brightly patterned cotton contrast with the black chadors of the townswomen. The nomad women's necklaces and bracelets often represent all their wealth and may include strings of very old silver and gold coins collected over the years.

As the tribes usually follow the same routes year after year, certain towns expect to see them travel through at the same time each year, bringing with them their special crafts to sell in the bazaars. Many of the most beautiful rugs made today come from the nomadic tribal groups.

Nomads moving to new
grazing grounds

A nomad woman and child
outside their tent

One of the double-headed stone bulls that used to support
the roof of Darius's palace at Persepolis

The King of Kings

In the early sixth century BC there were two main kingdoms in
what is now Iran—that of the Medes, in the northwest, and that
of the Farsis (a name later distorted into "Persians" by the
Greeks) in the west. In 553 BC Cyrus the Great, the king of the
Farsis and a member of the Achaemenid family, defeated the
Medes and combined their land with his own. Then, with his
powerful army, he conquered most of the then civilized world.
His empire stretched from the borders of Egypt in the west to
Central Asia in the east. He was the first great ruler of the
Persian Empire and the founder of the Achaemenid dynasty.
A dynasty is a succession of rulers all from the same line or family.

Darius the Great, the second great ruler of the Achaemenid
dynasty, reigned from 521 BC to 486 BC. His empire extended
into the north of India and to Greece. At home he built roads,
organized a postal service and introduced a fair system of

The tomb of Darius in the cliffs near Persepolis

One of the lion gateways of the palace

taxation. He established an efficient and lasting form of government. The king was supreme ruler (he was referred to as "The King of Kings", a title the present-day ruler still retains) and he governed the twenty-three provinces of the empire through carefully supervised officials called *satraps*.

The Persian emperors never tried to force Persian customs on their conquered peoples. Instead, Persia tended to borrow from each of its subject lands, particularly in art, architecture and technology. One of the masterpieces which resulted from this blending of foreign and Persian art was the Achaemenid capital, Persepolis. Darius built Persepolis as a symbol of the greatness of his empire. Artists and craftsmen were brought from Babylon, Egypt, Syria and Asia Minor to work on it, and materials came from all the lands of the empire. The main doors of the palaces and temples were of solid gold, statues were embellished with gold, and even the curtains were made of gold lace.

Persepolis is in ruins now, but, though none of the splendid decorations remain, one can still imagine the beauty that was there. Still standing are walls and columns which show the vast extent and scale of the buildings. The

A bas-relief of Darius on his throne, receiving the homage of a Mede officer

bas-reliefs, carved in stone on the walls and staircases, give a glimpse of life at Darius's court. For instance, in the audience hall Darius is shown sitting on his throne, attended by a servant carrying a fly whisk made from the tail of a bull. Dignitaries stand in front of him, guards stand in formation. On a staircase there is a procession bringing tribute to the king: groups from all the provinces of the empire, in national dress, carrying animals and gifts from their lands.

Later Achaemenid kings lost the lands that Cyrus and Darius had won, and in 331 BC their dynasty came to an end when Alexander the Great, the ruler of Macedon, conquered Persia. He was a great admirer of Persia. He married a Persian woman and encouraged his men to marry Persians too. He wanted the Greeks to learn from Persia, and so he ordered that great numbers of Persian books should be translated into Greek. This is why so much is known about early Persian history.

Despite Alexander's love for Persia it was during his campaign that Persepolis was burned and left in ruins. No one really knows how or why this tragedy occurred.

41

The Royal Mosque at Isfahan, built by Shah Abbas in the sixteenth century

Islamic Persia

After the fall of the Achaemenid dynasty and the death of Alexander in 323 BC, other dynasties ruled in Persia. At times Persia was able to extend its frontiers, but at other times the empire was under attack and lost territories. The nomad peoples of the Central Asian steppes to the northwest and the Arabs, a nomad people from across the Persian Gulf to the southwest, were constant threats.

In AD 651 Persia became part of the Arab empire and the people were converted to Islam. In time the great Arab empire broke up and Persia was ruled by other Muslim overlords (for instance, the Turks in the eleventh century and the Mongols in the thirteenth).

It was not until the sixteenth century that a leader appeared who was strong enough to reunite the country and to bring back some of its earlier glory. This leader was Shah Abbas the Great who ruled from 1586 to 1628. He defeated the Turks and Tatars, who were occupying parts of the country, and once again extended the boundaries of Persia. He was a great warrior, diplomat, administrator, builder, patron of the arts and sciences and, above all, a wise and tolerant ruler.

Within his lifetime Shah Abbas transformed the town of Isfahan into one of the most beautiful capitals of the day. At that time it had 162 mosques, 48 colleges and 1802 caravanserais (open courtyards which served as camping grounds for people on journeys). Much of the Isfahan built by Shah Abbas remains.

At the heart of the town is the Meydine Shah (the "Royal Square") or Nag e Jahan (meaning "image of the world"). At one end of this square is the Royal Mosque, one of the finest buildings in the world. The rich blue and gold of the intricate patterns which ornament the walls and domes are extremely beautiful. Inside there are peaceful courtyards with arcades and loggias.

At the opposite end of the square is the bazaar, which seems to spread endlessly, with side passages opening into little mosques.

A detail of the rich decoration in the Royal Mosque

A tribal battle

The Ali Qupu

The gateway of one of the many beautiful mosques in Shiraz

On the west side of the square is a building called the Ali Qupu, "sublime door". It was here that Shah Abbas and his successors entertained important foreign visitors. Here too the shah could sit on the balcony and observe his people. Military parades and polo matches (polo was a national sport) took place on the square below. The open square was also used as a camping ground for caravan trains from all over Asia. Much trading took place here as well as in the bazaar. Today the great square is empty except for wandering visitors.

For a brief period in the second half of the eighteenth century, under the Zand dynasty, Shiraz was the capital of Persia. The city was already famous as the birthplace of two of Persia's greatest poets, Hafez (born AD 1324) and Sa'adi (born AD 1190). It was famous too for its gardens and vineyards and so it was referred to as a "city of wine, roses and poets". The Zand rulers wanted to make Shiraz as beautiful as Isfahan and so they built several very lovely mosques and a handsome bazaar. The town and particularly the bazaar are often crowded with nomads who come into the city to buy supplies and sell their wares.

44

Iran in the Twentieth Century

In the early part of the twentieth century Europe and North America were making great technological advances, but these developments had hardly touched Persia at all. In 1921 Reza Khan, a former army officer, seized power and set about modernizing the country so that it could once again play a role as a world power. In 1925 he became the first shah of the Pahlavi dynasty. ("Pahlavi" is the name of the language and of the script used in Persia before the Arab conquest.)

His first step was to rename the country "Iran", "land of the Aryans", a name associated with the empire of Cyrus and Darius. This was to tell the world that the country was no longer a "fallen Persia" but a reborn, fast-growing nation. His next project was to build a new capital city. Tehran was chosen and work began to transform it into a modern, European-style city.

Like many of his predecessors, he had the final say in all decisions of government. His reign brought terror to many of his people, and others complained of the stifling atmosphere of his dictatorship. Iran, however, took huge steps towards becoming the country it is today.

LEFT Shah Reza, the soldier who founded the Pahlavi dynasty. RIGHT Iran is still under military rule and cabinet ministers are members of the army and train as soldiers

Tehran, the city Shah Reza chose as his capital. It lies close to the Elburz mountains

The daily lives of the people changed quite dramatically. The Shah felt that religion was hindering the modernization of the country, so he took steps to limit the power and influence of the mullahs. Shah Reza also ordered the men to substitute European suits, ties and hats for their traditional turbans and loose flowing robes. Women were forbidden to wear the veil and were encouraged to go out in public. In 1930 Shah Reza opened the mosques to non-Muslims so that, for instance, Christians might visit them.

Though Shah Reza built schools, hospitals and factories and also the Trans-Iranian Railway, a large part of the country's income was spent on the construction of magnificent government buildings and on a very strong army which was completely under the Shah's control. All these projects required money, and heavy and often unfair taxation was imposed on the people. The Shah's policies were not easily accepted and a number of groups and tribes rebelled, but by 1930 the Shah's army had pacified the

46

country. The Shah banned political parties with foreign links. Little concern was shown for the individual. There was no freedom of the press and little freedom of speech or of action.

Before Shah Reza came to power, there had been a long period of intervention in Persian affairs by foreign powers, particularly Russia and Britain. Foreign companies were deeply involved in setting up industries, in running railway, steamship and customs services and in training the army. Shah Reza renegotiated treaties and contracts so that Iranians took over these services.

Having removed Russian and British influences from his country, Shah Reza began to turn to Germany for technical help. When the Second World War (1939–45) broke out, Iran tried to remain neutral. Before long the Allies (Britain and the Soviet Union) needed Iran as a land bridge to carry supplies to the Soviet Union and as a source of oil. In 1941 they invaded Iran. The pro-German Shah Reza was forced to abdicate, and his son Muhammad succeeded him.

Iran does not yet have an up-to-date road system and the existing roads are very congested

The Shah's photograph is always present

Policewomen parade on the anniversary of the White Revolution

Muhammad Reza Shah, the present Shahanshah or "King of Kings", came to the throne in 1941, but it was not until 1967 that his coronation took place. In the years between becoming leader and his coronation, the Shah took strong measures to improve the country. During the Second World War the Iranian people had suffered greatly from lack of supplies and enormous rises in prices. They had been humiliated by the occupation of their country, but, having seen foreign troops running transport and communications services, they had been left with an awareness of how more developed societies worked. When the war ended and foreign troops withdrew, Iran could concentrate on her internal problems.

Despite the reforms and attempts at modernization undertaken by Shah Reza, conditions for the majority of Iranians had remained very primitive. All the land was in the hands of a few wealthy and powerful families. The people who worked on the land had no rights in it, and a proportion of their crops had to go to the owners of the land.

A major step towards reform was taken by Shah Muhammad

48

with the launching in 1963 of "The White Revolution", officially called "The Revolution of the Shahanshah and the Nation". Its first aim was the redistribution of land, taking land from the great landowners and giving it to the peasants who worked it. The Pahlavi Dynasty Trust was set up to provide income for social, educational and health services.

While Shah Reza had attempted to modernize the country by restricting the influence of the Muslim religion, Shah Muhammad tried a different approach. He allowed the religion to flourish again and women were no longer forbidden to wear the veil. The Shah took active steps, however, to improve the status of women. In 1963 they were allowed to vote for the first time. At his coronation in 1967 he did something unheard of in a Muslim country—he placed a crown on his wife's head. Ever since then, his wife, Empress Farah, has openly encouraged the women of Iran to take an active role in society.

The Shah and Empress Farah in their coronation robes, with their son

The Shah visits a nomad school in a tent

Today, women, though still not always allowed full equality with men, are attending universities and taking jobs previously reserved for men.

National life is focused on the Shah and the Royal Family and there are photographs of them everywhere, in shops, houses and public places, as well as in the daily papers.

The Shah commands the army and this, as in the days of his father, remains the most powerful force in Iran, controlling the police, the passport service, the corps of young people working to improve conditions in the villages and also the secret police. Everyone knows that the Shah is the supreme leader and no one is allowed to criticize him or his policies. Iranians are very careful not to let their real political views be known if these differ from those of the government. The secret police force is very powerful and anyone might be an agent—a taxi-driver, a shopkeeper or a passer-by. People who disagree in public with

The Shahyad Tower, built as a tribute to the Pahlavi dynasty in 1971

A new steel mill in Isfahan

Royal enthusiasm for skiing is copied by many

government policy might be considered, rightly or wrongly, to be dangerous to the state.

The industrialization of Iran has grown at an enormous rate. Today the country is moving into the heavy goods industries of steel and copper, machine tools, petrochemicals and car manufacture.

New office buildings, factories, schools, universities, hospitals and hotels are just some of the surface changes in Iran. The real changes which must take place in order to modernize a country completely do not happen overnight, or even over fifty years. While today Tehran and other major cities of Iran already look like similar jet-age cities all over the world, large areas of the country are still just emerging from the past. Tractors are replacing horses and oxen, cars are taking the place of camels and carts, but the people's attitudes are far more difficult to change. Many do not want their lives to be altered by European and American ideas and machines but prefer to continue their own traditions and customs. They do not feel that new technologies necessarily suit Iran. The country will probably take many years to find a happy balance between old and new.

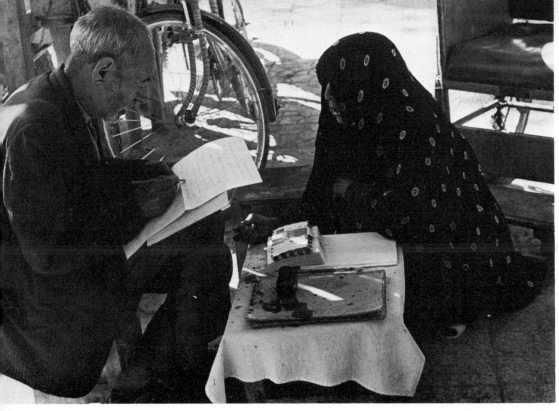

A professional letter writer

Education

One of the important aims of the White Revolution is to educate the people of Iran. Shah Muhammad Reza feels strongly that the growth and development of the country depend on the education of its people. Illiteracy is still high, but this is because most of the older generation never had the chance to learn to read and write, and many of the younger people have still not found a place in a school. It is quite common to see "writers" sitting in public places, taking down letters for people who cannot themselves read or write.

Today government schools offer free primary education to children aged from six to twelve, and it is intended that one day even the most remote village should have a school. Schools and universities have been opening at a tremendous rate over the past years, yet there are still not enough to meet the demand.

Even though in theory education is compulsory between the ages of six and twelve, many children can be seen working in the bazaars and in shops. It is obvious that it will take time to enforce this law and that meanwhile many children are not sent to school but are educated by helping their parents to run a business.

The Iranian school year is not divided into terms. School begins in September and goes right through to June, with only a two-week holiday in March for the Iranian New Year. The school week begins at eight o'clock on Saturday morning and ends at midday on Thursday. This leaves half a day free on Thursday and all day on Friday, the Muslim day of prayer. The school day lasts from eight in the morning until four in the afternoon.

In the past the few schools there were concentrated on calligraphy and on studying the scriptures. This meant learning to recite long passages of the Koran in Arabic. Although present-day schools

Off to school

Schoolgirls coming out of school. Some wear *chadors*, some don't

Primary-school children sit quietly at rows of desks

A young boy working in a carpet factory

offer a full range of subjects and use modern textbooks similar to those used in America and Europe, the methods of teaching and learning are still influenced by the old religious schools. The teacher has total authority and expects the students to listen and learn, not to discuss and question. Much of the learning is still done by memorizing the lessons.

An important subject on the school time-table is Farsi, the official language of Iran. In origin it is an Indo-European language and belongs to the same family of languages as English, French, German, Russian and many others. Farsi exists in two different versions, one for speaking and one for writing. The spoken language is used in everyday conversation and has changed and evolved over the years.

The written language is very different from the spoken one and is used by educated people only. It has remained unchanged since the eleventh century when the famous poet Firdowsi wrote a legendary history of Persia in fifty thousand couplets, *The Book of Kings*. The form used by the poet has been the basis of the written language ever since.

At the end of the primary-school course, at the age of eleven or twelve, students who pass a major examination may go on to high school until they are sixteen or seventeen. In many high schools up to twelve subjects are studied at a time, and at the end of each year the students have an examination in each one. A failure in one subject means that the student must repeat the entire year.

Since there are still not enough schools and universities in Iran, many students are sent by the government to schools in Europe and America. Before they leave to study abroad, they must guarantee that they will return to Iran.

It is compulsory for all men to serve in the army at some time. For those who have been to high school, army service can be replaced in part by national service which can be done at any time between the ages of eighteen and thirty-five.

The first six months of national service are spent in military training. The remaining eighteen months are devoted to various

The courtyard of a theological college in Isafahan. It was built *c.* 1710 to train mullahs and is still in use

A nursery-school class run by the Literacy Corps

A Literacy Corps teacher with her class

A Health Corps student putting up posters in a village clinic

government social development plans. Many students spend their national service time working for the Literacy Corps which was set up by the Shah as a way of teaching reading and writing to the poorly educated. The aim of the Literacy Corps is to bring education into the remote villages. Schools are set up to educate both the young and the old. These schools teach trades such as weaving and pottery making as well as basic reading and writing.

Students who have medical training join the Health Corps and work in clinics where basic hygiene and birth control are taught to the villagers.

Under this system of national service each graduating student has the opportunity to use the education received from the state to help raise the general standard of living in the remote areas of the country. Today women are being encouraged to volunteer for national service. Thus all are involved in improving their own country.

Oil

Few of the Pahlavi dynasty's plans could have been carried out, were it not for the vast amount of money which Iranian oil has brought to the country.

Oil has been a part of Persian life since the earliest days. Liquid oil and escaping gases came to the surface from the oil-bearing beds which lay deep under the ground. These gases and oil patches were sometimes ignited by lightning and would burst into flames. People were amazed by these unexpected fires and began to worship them. When Zoroastrianism became the official religion of the Achaemenids, fire temples with eternal flames were built. Sometimes these temples were over or close to a gas or oil escape spring.

It was not until modern times that oil was considered a valuable commodity. In 1901 an Englishman, hearing of the oil deposits in Persia, obtained permission from the Persian government to prospect for oil. He found oil and in 1909 sold his rights to the newly founded Anglo-Persian Oil Company. Britain has played an important role in helping Iran to develop the oil industry. During the First and Second World Wars the oil provided British ships with fuel.

An oil rig in a remote mountain area in southern Iran

Part of the giant refinery at Abadan

After the Second World War the Shahanshah decided that the money earned from oil sales should be reinvested in developing new industries in Iran, so he nationalized the oil company and renamed it the National Iranian Oil Company. Today the company administers the oil industry and British, American, French and Dutch companies have money invested in the industry. The National Iranian Oil Company is the second largest oil producer and exporter in the Middle East. It handles all aspects of the oil industry, including refining, transport, distribution and petrochemical manufacture.

The world's largest—and one of the most modern—refineries is at Abadan, an Iranian town on the Persian Gulf.

Chosen as the site for a refinery in 1910, it soon became the Middle East's first industrial city. Today the refinery covers an area of five square miles (13 km²) and an additional nineteen square miles (49 km²) are used for the housing and community services for those who work in the oil industry. Within this area are schools, hospitals, shops and extensive facilities for sports and recreation.

When oil comes out of the ground, it is in a form called "crude oil". Oil consists of atoms of hydrogen and carbon, linked together in molecules. But there are a number of different patterns of molecule. Some form a thick, heavy liquid. Others are light and turn easily into gas. In crude oil all these molecules are mingled together. Before the oil can be used, the molecules must be sorted into their different types by a process called "refining".

When the crude oil reaches the refinery from the oil field, it is heated to a temperature above 600°F (315°C) and is fed into distillation units. The heaviest molecules, which do not turn into gas at this temperature, remain as liquid at the bottom of the distillation unit. The lighter molecules rise to different heights in the distillation column, according to their weights.

Iranian oil is carried to other parts of the world in supertankers

Complex machinery is operated from this central control room in the Abadan refinery

Once the molecules have been sorted in this way, the different types of oil can be drawn off. This first process results in six main divisions: raw gasoline or petrol, naphtha, kerosene or paraffin, gas oil (diesel fuel), fuel oil and bitumen.

After this initial separation each of these "cuts" is further divided into other products. While most refineries may produce up to forty different products from crude oil, Abadan can produce well over a hundred. High-grade specialized products are exported to many parts of the world.

The refinery is run by an intricate computer system. Among the forests of chimney stacks and weirdly shaped piping systems there is hardly a man to be seen, for all the machinery is con-

trolled from central offices:
many machines and few people,
all working very, very efficient-
ly to create great wealth for
the country as a whole.

Today oil is Iran's largest
and most important industry.
But the country is also well
aware that, just as the fire
temples of the days of Zoroaster
disappeared, one day so will
the oil.

Determined that his coun-
try's economic power shall not
disappear when the oil deposits
are exhausted, the Shahanshah
has developed huge nuclear
power stations and an iron and
steel industry as a carefully
planned investment for his
country's future.

Pipes carry the different products
of the refining process

Modern Iran and ancient Persia: the tall stacks of the Abadan refinery
echo the pillars of Persepolis

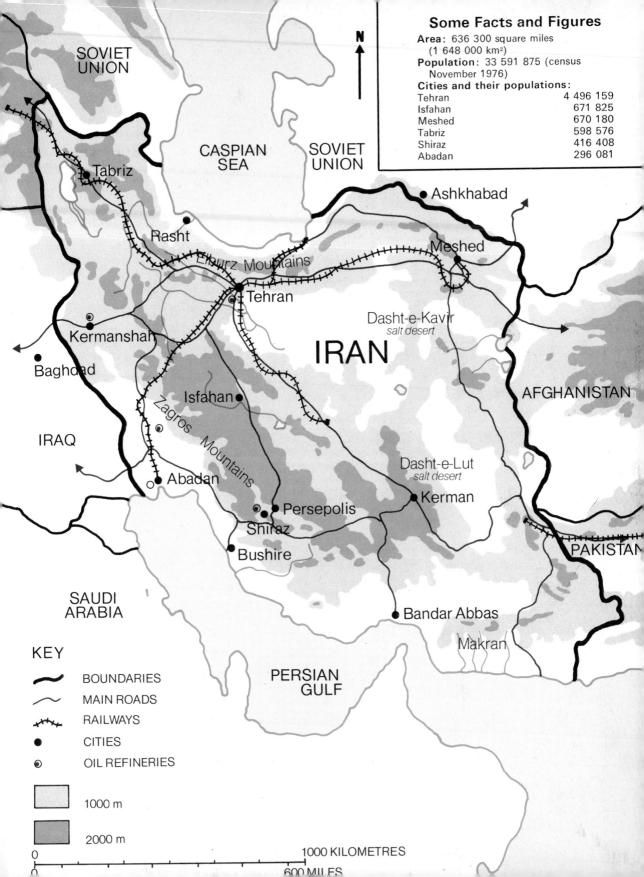

N

Some Facts and Figures

Area: 636 300 square miles
(1 648 000 km²)
Population: 33 591 875 (census
November 1976)
Cities and their populations:

Tehran	4 496 159
Isfahan	671 825
Meshed	670 180
Tabriz	598 576
Shiraz	416 408
Abadan	296 081

SOVIET
UNION

CASPIAN
SEA

SOVIET
UNION

● Ashkhabad

Tabriz

Rasht

Elburz Mountains

Meshed

Tehran

Dasht-e-Kavir
salt desert

IRAN

Kermanshah

AFGHANISTAN

Baghdad

Zagros

Isfahan

Mountains

IRAQ

Dasht-e-Lut
salt desert

Abadan

Kerman

Persepolis

Shiraz

Bushire

PAKISTAN

SAUDI
ARABIA

Bandar Abbas

Makran

KEY

PERSIAN
GULF

〜 BOUNDARIES

〜 MAIN ROADS

╫╫╫ RAILWAYS

● CITIES

◉ OIL REFINERIES

☐ 1000 m

☐ 2000 m

0   1000 KILOMETRES

0   600 MILES

Index